ŠEVČÍK
Op. 9

PREPARATORY STUDIES IN DOUBLE-STOPPING

DOPPELGRIFF-VORSTUDIEN
EXERCICES PRÉPARATOIRES DE DOUBLES NOTES

for

VIOLA
(ALTO)

arranged / bearbeitet / arrangées
by   von   par

Alan Arnold

Bosworth

SEVCIK Op. 9 FOR VIOLA
arr. Alan Arnold

EXERCISES IN DOUBLE-STOPPING

Each exercise, both in its original and varied forms, is to be practiced in the following keys, with particular observance of the different detached and legato bowings.

DOPPELGRIFF ÜBUNGEN

Man übe jedes Beispiel und jede Variante in den folgenden Tonarten, unter genauer Beachtung der abgesetzen oder gebundenen Stricharten.

EXERCICES EN DOUBLES CORDES

Chaque exercice aussi bien dans sa forme originale et variée doit être pratiqué dans les tons suivants en observant particulièrement les différents détachés et legato de l'archet.

1.

OCTAVES (See note to Op. 8)

OKTAVEN (Siehe Anmerkung zu Op. 8)

OCTAVES (Voir la remarque de Op. 8)

Varied forms:
Varianten:
Variantes:

2.

1) In G♭ and C♭, the first and last measure of these exercises are omitted.

1) In Ges und Ces entfällt in der Übung der erste und letzte Takt.

1) En sol♭ et en do♭ on ne joue pas la première et la dernière mesure des exemples.

B. & Co. Ltd. 22279

3.

SIXTHS   SEXTEN   SIXTES

4.

5.

THIRDS   TERZEN   TIERCES

etc.

6.

etc.

7.

FOURTHS   QUARTEN   QUARTES

etc.

4

8.

9.

10.

*Do not raise the 2nd and 3rd fingers.   *Den 2. und 3. Finger nicht heben.   *Ne levez pas le *2me* et le *3me* doigt.

5

11.

SIXTHS   SEXTEN   SIXTES

12.

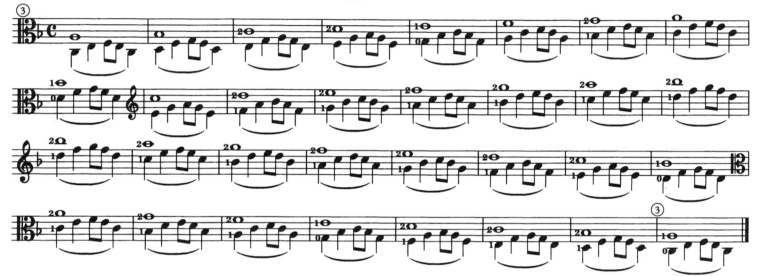

13.

14.

THIRDS   TERZEN   TIERCES

15.

16.

SECONDS   SEKUNDEN   SECONDES

17.

FOURTHS   QUARTEN   QUARTES

18.

19.

OCTAVES   OKTAVEN   OCTAVES

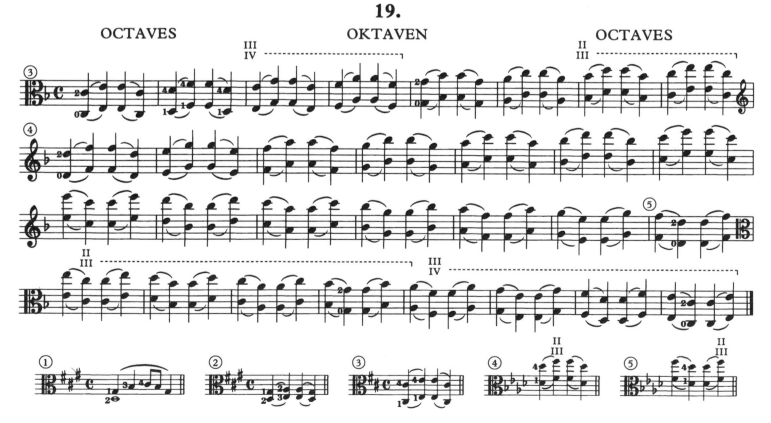

8

20.

21.

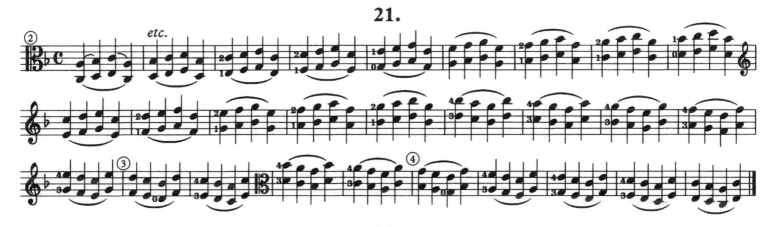

22.

SIXTHS   SEXTEN   SIXTES

23.

24.

THIRDS   **TERZEN**   **TIERCES**

25.

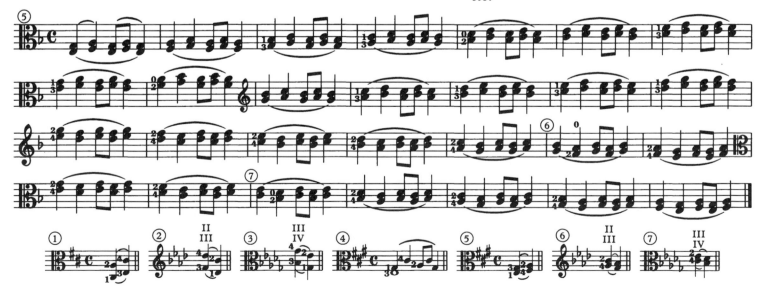

26.

FOURTHS QUARTEN QUARTES

27.

28.

TENTHS

Exercise caution in the preparation of this study. If the violist has a small hand and/or an excessively large viola, great care must be taken to find a comfortable and relaxed hand position. Pain is a warning signal to stop immediately.

DEZIMEN

Vorsicht beim Spielen dieser Übungen! Wenn die Hand des Bratschisten sehr klein oder die Bratsche übermäßig groß ist, achte man besonders auf eine bequeme und entspannte Handstellung. Bei Auftreten von Schmertzen das Spiel sofort unterbrechen.

DIXIEMES

Veuillez à être prudent dans la préparation de cette étude. Si l'altiste a la main petite ou un instrument particulièrement grand, il faut faire attention à ce que la position de la main soit confortable et relachée. A partir du moment où l'on ressent une peine, il faut arrêter immédiatement.

29.

32.

33.

THIRDS   **TERZEN**   **TIERCES**

34.

35.

36.

SECONDS   SEKUNDEN   SECONDES

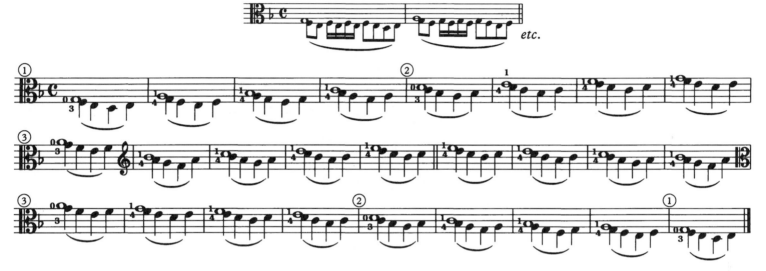

37.

FOURTHS   QUARTEN   QUARTES

38.

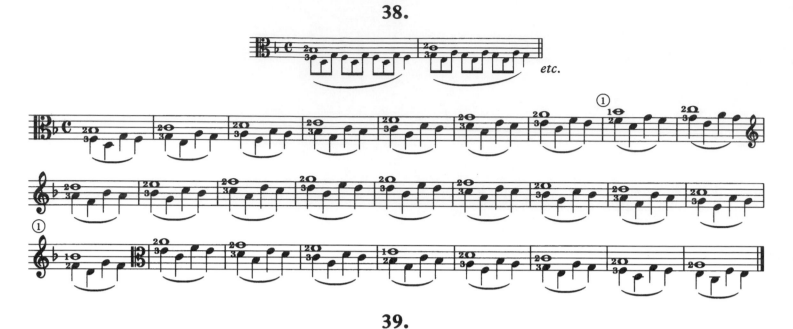

39.

*TENTHS   ***DEZIMEN**   ***DIXIEMES**

40.

OCTAVES   **OKTAVEN**   **OCTAVES**

* See note, page 11   *Siehe Anmerkung Seite 11   *Voir la remarque de la page 11

41.

42.

SIXTHS　　　　　SEXTEN　　　　　SIXTES

43.

16

44.

THIRDS　　　　TERZEN　　　　TIERCES

45.

etc.

46.

FOURTHS　　　　QUARTEN　　　　QUARTES

47.

48.

*TENTHS   *DEZIMEN   *DIXIEMES

49.

SIXTHS   SEXTEN   SIXTES

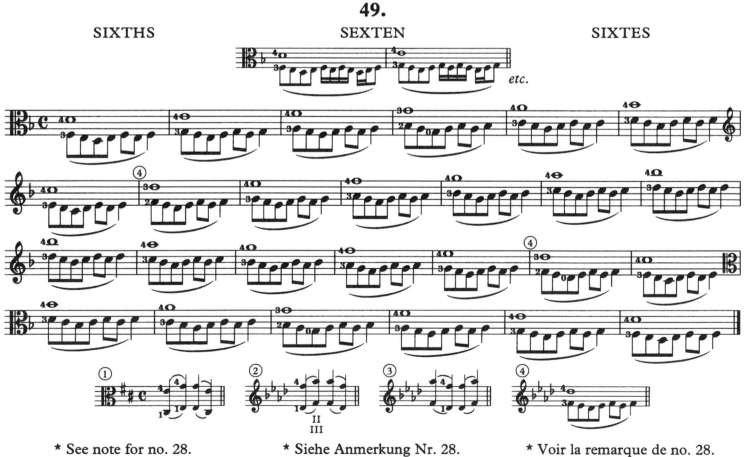

* See note for no. 28. * Siehe Anmerkung Nr. 28. * Voir la remarque de no. 28.

B. & Co. Ltd. 22279

50.

OCTAVES OKTAVEN OCTAVES

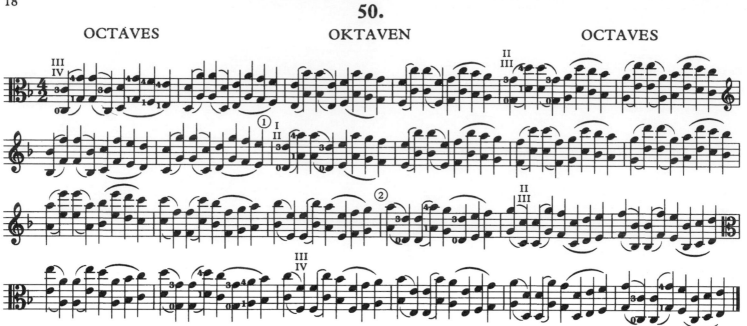

51.

FOURTHS QUARTEN QUARTES

52.

SIXTHS SEXTEN SIXTES

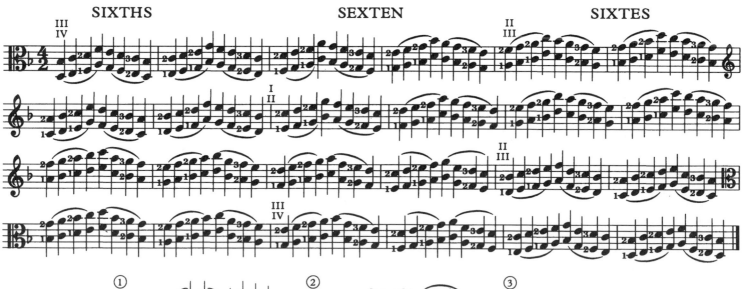

53.

★54.

55.

56.

57.

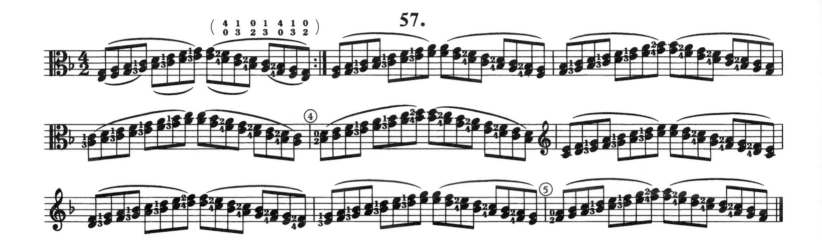

58.

HARMONICS   FLAGEOLETT   SONS HARMONIQUES

simile

VIOLA WORLD

PUBLISHERS OF MUSIC FOR THE SERIOUS VIOLIST

Studies

ARNOLD, Alan
3-Octave Scales & Arpeggios
BLUMENSTENGAL, A.
Viola Scale Technique Bk.1 - 1st Pos.
Viola Scale Technique Bk.2 -1-5 Pos.
HOFMANN, Richard
Melodic Double-Stop Studies Op. 96
TARTINI, Giuseppe
The Art of Bowing

Viola Solo

ARNOLD, Alan
Cadenzas for Telemann Viola Concerto
KREISLER, Fritz
Recitative and Scherzo Caprice
WOEHR, Christian
Bachiana

Viola & Piano Albums

ARNOLD, Alan
The Young Violist Bk. 1 (easy pieces)
The Young Violist Bk. 2 (more pieces)
BACH, J.S.
Basic Bach (arr.Arnold)
BEETHOVEN, Ludwig van
Beethoven's Best (arr. Arnold)
MOZART, W.A
Mozart Miniatures (arr. Arnold)

Viola & Piano Repertoire

BACH, J.S.
Bourrée in C minor
Chromatic Fantasy and Fugue
BEETHOVEN, Ludwig van
Für Elise
BENJAMIN, Arthur
Jamaican Rumba
BOCCHERINI, Luigi
Music Box Minuet
BÖHM, Carl
Sarabande
BOROWSKI, Felix
Adoration
BRAHMS, Johannes
Scherzo
CHOPIN, Frédéric
Nocturne
CORELLI, Arcangelo
Sarabande, Giga and Badinerie
Sonata No.12 - La Folia con Variazione

DANCLA, Charles
Carnival of Venice
DE BÉRIOT, Ch.
Scène de Ballet
DEBUSSY, Claude
Girl with the Flaxen Hair
La Plus Que Lente
DVORÁK, Antonin
Romance Op. 11
Sonatina Op. 100
FAURÉ, Gabriel
Fantasie
FIOCCO, Gioseffo-Hectore
Allegro
FRANCOEUR, François
Sonata in A
GLUCK, Christoff W. von
Melody from *Orfeo ed Euridice*
HANDEL, G.F.
Bourrée
Concerto in B flat
Sonata in B flat
Sonata in D
HUBAY, Jenö
Hejre Kati
JENKINSON, Ezra
Elves' Dance (*Elfentanz*)
JOPLIN, Scott
Pineapple Rag
Solace
KREISLER, Fritz
Liebesfreud
Liebesleid
Praeludium and Allegro
Sicilienne and Rigaudon
MASSENET, Jules
Meditation from *Thaïs*
MATTHEWS, Holon
Fantasy
MENDELSSOHN, Felix
Sonata in E flat
MOZART, W.A.
Adagio K.261
Menuetto Divertimento K.334
Rondo K.250
Serenata Cantabile
MUSSORGSKY, Modest
Hopak
NOVACEK, Ottokar
Perpetual Motion
PAGANINI, Niccolò
Six Sonatas Bk. 1, Nos 1, 2, 3
Six Sonatas Bk. 2, Nos 4, 5, 6
Variations on the G-String
PUGNANI, Gaetano
Gavotta Variata

RACHMANINOFF, Sergei
Vocalise
RIES, Franz
Perpetuum Mobile
RIMSKY-KORSAKOV, N.
Flight of the Bumble Bee
SCHMIDT, Ernst
Alla Turca
SHUBERT, Franz
The Bee
TARTINI, Giuseppe
Sonata angelique
The Devil's Trill
TCHAIKOVSKY, P.
Canzonetta
June Barcarolle
Mélodie
Sérénade mélancholique
Valse sentimentale
VITALI, Giovanni
Chaconne
VIVALDI, Antonio
Sonata in G
WEBER, Carl M.
Andante and Hungarian Rondo
WIENIAWSKI, Henryk
Légende
Scherzo Tarantella

Viola Duos

BACH, J. S.
Fifteen Two-Part Inventions
MOZART, W.A.
Duo Sonata in B flat K.292
Twelve Duets K.487

3 Violas & Piano

PACHELBEL, Johann
Canon

4 Violas

TELEMANN, Georg Philipp
Concerto No. 1 in C for 4 Violas
Concerto No. 2 in G for 4 Violas
Concerto No. 3 in F for 4 Violas
Concerto No. 4 in D for 4 Violas

4 Violas & Piano

VIVALDI, Antonio
Concerto for 4 Violas and Piano

Available from:

Bosworth